PULL AHEAD BOOKS
Forces of Nature

Northern Lights

by Janet Piehl

Lerner

Lerner Books • London • New York • Minneapolis

For Caitlin, Nicolai, and Amalia

Photo Acknowledgements

The images in this book are used with the permission of: © Photodisc/Getty Images, all backgrounds, p15; © age fotostock/SuperStock, p 4; © Per-Andre Hoffmann/LOOK Die Bildagentur der Fotografen GmbH/Alamy, pp 6, 10; © Iconica/ Arctic-Images/Getty Images, pp 7, 25; © iStockphoto.com/Roman Krochuk, pp 8, 11, 16; © Ron Niebrugge/ Alamy, p 9; NASA-JPL, p 12; © Koji Kitagawa/SuperStock, p 14; © Gerald & Buff Corsi/Visuals Unlimited, p 17; © Phil Degginger/Alamy, p 18; © Taxi/World Perspectives/Getty Images, p 20; © Doug Allan/The Image Bank/Getty Images, p 21; © Astrofoto/Peter Arnold, Inc., p 22; © Rolf Hicker/All Canada Photos/Alamy, p 24; © Aurora/ Joel Sheagren/Getty Images, p 26; © Stuart O'Sullivan/Stone/Getty Images, p 27. Illustrations on pp 19, 28 by © Laura Westlund/Independent Picture Service.

Front cover: © Kevin Schafer/Photographer's Choice/Getty Images.
Back cover: © Photodisc/Getty Images.

First published in the United Kingdom in 2010 by
Lerner Books,
Dalton House,
60 Windsor Avenue,
London SW19 2RR

Website address: www.lernerbooks.co.uk

This edition was updated and edited for UK publication by Discovery Books Ltd., First Floor, 2 College Street, Ludlow, Shropshire SY8 1AN

Words in **bold type** are explained in a glossary on page 31.

British Library Cataloguing in Publication Data

Piehl, Janet
Northern lights. - 2nd ed. - (Pull ahead books. Forces of nature)
1. Auroras - Juvenile literature
I. Title
538.7'68

ISBN-13: 978 0 7613 4392 9

Printed in China

Table of Contents

What Are the Northern Lights?

The northern night sky glows green. A cloud of bright light drifts across the sky. The light changes shape and colour. Red rays flicker. What is happening?

The **northern lights** are out. The northern lights are a natural light show. They can be green, blue, yellow, red, pink or purple.

The northern lights appear in many different shapes.

Sometimes the northern lights look curved.

Sometimes they look like curtains or clouds. Other times, they look like ribbons or rays.

The northern lights happen more than 97 kilometres (60 miles) above the ground.

They stretch for thousands of
kilometres across the northern sky.

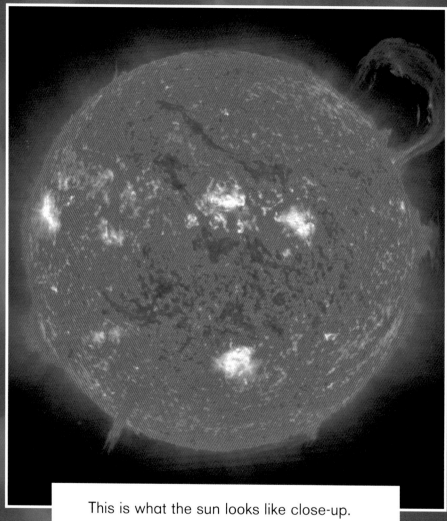

This is what the sun looks like close-up.

What Causes the Northern Lights?

The beginnings of the northern lights are at the sun. **Particles** stream out from the sun. The particles travel very fast through space. But the Earth is far away from the sun. The particles take two or three days to reach the Earth.

Earth's atmosphere as seen from space

The particles enter the Earth's **atmosphere**. The atmosphere is a layer of **gases** that surrounds the Earth.

14

The particles meet the gases in the atmosphere. They give off light when they meet. The lights are called **auroras**.

Auroras forming in the Earth's atmosphere

Auroras in the northern sky are called northern lights.

Auroras over the northern state of Alaska in the USA

But why are these lights in the
northern sky?

Imagine that the Earth is a **magnet**. A magnet pulls certain metal objects towards it. The Earth also pulls objects towards it.

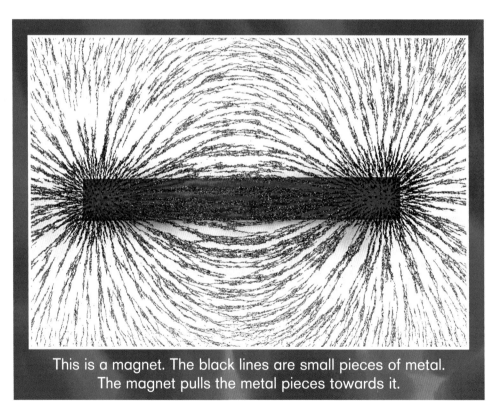

This is a magnet. The black lines are small pieces of metal. The magnet pulls the metal pieces towards it.

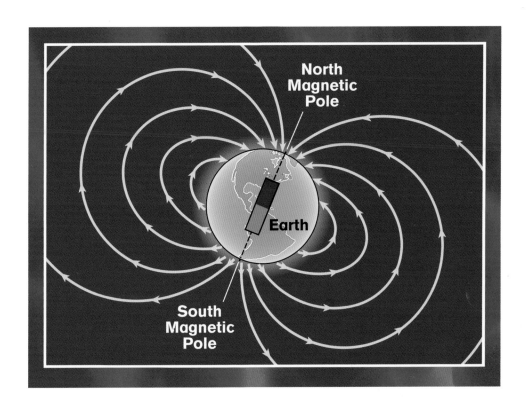

The Earth's **magnetic pull** is strongest near the North Pole and the South Pole. Particles from the sun are pulled towards the poles.

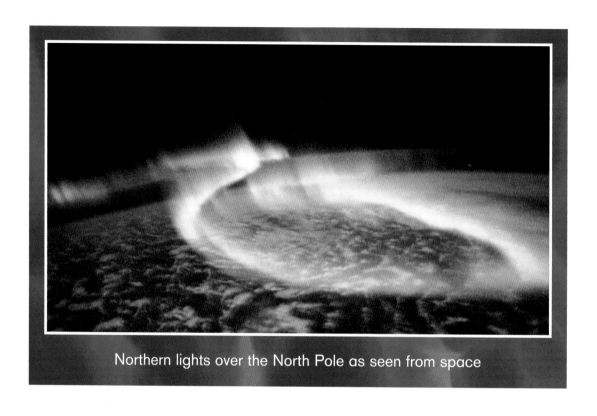

Northern lights over the North Pole as seen from space

The particles react with the Earth's atmosphere. Auroras form near the Earth's poles. The northern lights are auroras near the North Pole.

Auroras near the South Pole are called **southern lights**.

Southern lights over the continent of Antarctica

Northern lights glow above a town in Norway.

Where and When to See the Northern Lights

People in countries like Norway, Sweden, Finland, Russia and Canada often see the northern lights. In Alaska, people often see them, too. People sometimes see them in the USA and in parts of the UK.

Northern lights in spring over Canada

The best months to see the northern lights are September, October, March and April.

Northern lights are present during the day. But you can only see them at night when the sky is dark.

The northern lights are best seen around midnight.

What do you see in the northern night sky?

MORE ABOUT THE NORTHERN LIGHTS

This map shows where the northern lights can be seen in Europe, North America and the Arctic.

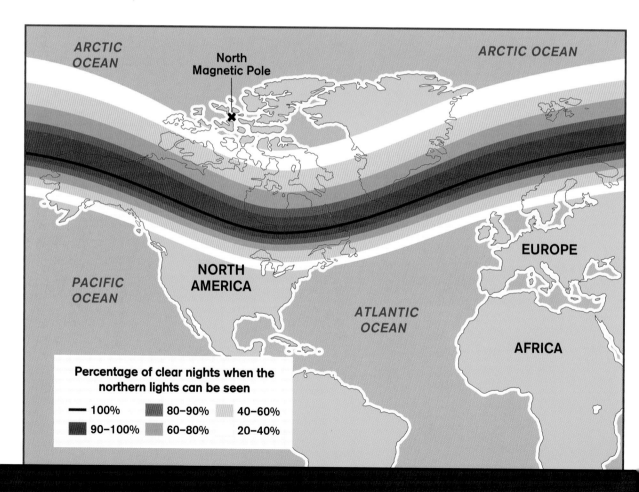

ARCTIC OCEAN

North Magnetic Pole

ARCTIC OCEAN

X

PACIFIC OCEAN

NORTH AMERICA

ATLANTIC OCEAN

EUROPE

AFRICA

Percentage of clear nights when the northern lights can be seen

— 100%   80–90%   40–60%

90–100%   60–80%   20–40%

Northern Lights Facts

• Another way to say 'northern lights' is 'aurora borealis'. That is Latin for 'northern dawn'. Another way to say 'southern lights' is 'aurora australis'. This means 'southern dawn'.

• Many people say they hear sounds when they see the northern lights. But scientists have not been able to prove that the sounds are real.

• People have told many stories to explain the northern lights. People in Finland thought that a fox running through the mountains made the northern lights. Some Native American groups thought the northern lights were fires burning in the sky.

• A Norwegian scientist named Kristian Birkeland made many important discoveries about the northern lights in the early 1900s. His work has helped scientists to understand the northern lights.

Further Reading

Books

Bailey, Jacqui. *What Does a Magnet Do?* (Investigating Science) Franklin Watts, 2005.

Cooper, Christopher. *Magnetism* (Science Answers) Heinemann Library, 2003.

Goldstein, Margaret J. *The Sun* (Our Universe) Lerner Books, 2008.

Goldstein, Margaret J. *The Earth* (Our Universe) Lerner Books, 2008.

Websites

AuroraWatch
http://www.dcs.lancs.ac.uk/iono/aurorawatch
Read information about the northern lights in the UK, including when they can be seen. This website also has a gallery of photographs taken around the UK.

BBC Weather – Northern Lights
http://www.bbc.co.uk/weather/features/understanding/northernlights.shtml
This webpage contains general information about the northern lights, such as how they are formed and where they occur.

Virtual Finland: Aurora Borealis
http://www.virtual.finland.fi/Nature_Environment/aurora/index.html
Watch videos of the northern lights and read information about them.

Glossary

atmosphere: the layer of gases that surrounds the Earth

auroras: a special kind of light that can sometimes be seen in the night sky. Auroras appear most often near the Earth's poles.

gases: substances, such as air, that can change size or shape

magnet: an object that pulls certain metal objects towards it. Magnets are often made of metal themselves.

magnetic pull: a magnet's power to bring objects towards it

northern lights: the glow in the sky that appears close to the North Pole

particles: tiny pieces

southern lights: the glow in the sky that appears close to the South Pole

Index

First published in the United States of America in 2009
Text copyright © 2009 by Lerner Publishing Group, Inc.